T0304379

Health Shots

50 Simple Tonics to
Help Improve Immunity, Ease Anxiety,
Boost Energy, and More

Toby Amidor, RD

WORKMAN PUBLISHING · NEW YORK

Before beginning any change in your health regimen, consult a professional health-care
practitioner. Neither the author nor the publisher shall be liable or responsible for any
loss, injury, or damage allegedly arising from any information or suggestions in this book.

Workman
Workman Publishing
Hachette Book Group, Inc.
1290 Avenue of the Americas
New York, NY 10104
workman.com

Workman is an imprint of Workman Publishing, a division of Hachette Book Group, Inc.
The Workman name and logo are registered trademarks of Hachette Book Group, Inc.

Design by Galen Smith
Cover photo by Leesa Renae

The publisher is not responsible for websites (or their content) that are not owned
by the publisher.

Workman books may be purchased in bulk for business, educational, or promotional use.
For information, please contact your local bookseller or the Hachette Book Group Special
Markets Department at special.markets@hbgusa.com.

Library of Congress Cataloging-in-Publication Data is available
ISBN 978-1-5235-2884-4

First Edition November 2024
Printed in China on responsibly sourced paper.

10 9 8 7 6 5 4 3 2 1

To my beautiful children,
Schoen, Ellena, and Micah.
I love you most.

Contents

Chapter 1

What Health Shots Can Do for You

Congratulations on choosing to make your own health shots! Also known as tonics, health shots are powerful combinations of foods and/or beverages that have been linked to specific health benefits and made into drinks. Often, the ingredients provide compounds such as vitamins, minerals, and phytonutrients (natural plant compounds) that have been shown to help support various functions in your body. A health tonic isn't a magic cure, but it can help fill nutrient gaps by providing vitamins and/or minerals you may be lacking in your diet. When the nutrients in tonics are consumed regularly, they can help your body function at its peak.

On recent trips to the supermarket, I have seen small single-serving bottles of health tonics, all being sold for a pretty penny. Most of these premade tonics are made with simple ingredients you can easily find at the supermarket, and then minimally processed. For my recipes, I intentionally call for ingredients you can find at most supermarkets to create fifty tasty tonics that can be whipped up quickly.

Benefits of Homemade Tonics

There are numerous benefits to making your own tonics and consuming them regularly. Their components contain nutrients that have been linked to alleviating or improving certain health conditions or symptoms. For example, increased anthocyanin consumption has been linked to helping improve memory and cognition. Anthocyanins are found in berries, grapes, and apples, and that is why you will find a recipe for Mixed-Berry Brain Booster (page 51) in the chapter on brain health tonics. For each recipe, you will find a list of nutrients for which studies show some influence on a specific health issue or symptom. Sometimes it's one nutrient, and other times it can be four or five.

Making your own tonics means you control the ingredients. If you dislike or are allergic to one ingredient, many recipes offer swap suggestions in "Tonic Tips." In addition, once you buy the ingredients, you'll have enough to make four to six servings, which is more cost effective than purchasing a single 2- or 4-ounce (60 or 125 ml) tonic at a time. My recipes make several 2-ounce (60 ml) shots so you can double your serving or store some of it. Feel free to halve or double the recipes as you choose. When it comes to health shots, more isn't necessarily better, plus drinking a full recipe or two at a time may add unneeded calories to your day. Instead, enjoy up to half the recipe in a day.

Nutrients in Common Foods

A healthy eating plan consists of a variety of foods including whole grains, fruits, vegetables, lean protein, healthy fats, beans, peas, lentils, nuts, seeds, and milk and other dairy products. Herbs and spices are great not only for adding flavor; many also provide beneficial nutrients or compounds. For example, turmeric provides a powerful anti-inflammatory called curcumin. Ginger also provides phenolic compounds such as gingerol, which functions as an antioxidant and anti-inflammatory, and can also help fight certain harmful microbes in the body. Parsley provides antioxidants known as flavonoids.

At the beginning of each chapter, you will find an overview of the health issue being addressed. You will also find a list of nutrients that have been linked to helping that particular issue and the foods they can be found in. In addition to the listed nutrients, every tonic contains other good-for-you ingredients as well. Adding these homemade tonics to a basically healthy diet can help fill gaps in nutrients you may be missing. These chapters are not meant to diagnose or treat any health condition. Please consult your health-care provider if you have health concerns.

Food Safety Guidelines and Storage

When making tonics, you will be handling a lot of fresh fruits and vegetables. Always wash your hands thoroughly with soap and water before starting to handle ingredients. Any sliced leftover fruits or vegetables should be covered or wrapped and stored in the refrigerator immediately after use. If you make the same tonic recipe within about a week, you can use the remaining ingredients to help avoid food waste.

If you make a recipe that yields four or six shots, you can drink half and store half. Store shots individually or in one

large batch, covered tightly and refrigerated for up to four days (a Mason jar with a tight-fitting lid is good for storage). If you plan on toting your refrigerated shot to work or outside, an insulated container may be a good idea. Label and date the tonic so you know which one it is and be aware of its shelf life. You may want to make a few different tonics in advance, especially if you have a busy week or want to take them to work daily. Do not leave the shots at room temperature for more than two hours—and if the temperature is above 90°F (32°C), make that one hour. If you take a shot to work, store it in the refrigerator when you arrive.

To get optimal nutrients, tonics are best consumed soon after being made. Some nutrients decrease the longer they are exposed to air/oxygen. A handful of recipes recommend refrigerating your tonic for up to two hours before drinking because they taste better cold, but feel free to drink them sooner if you choose.

You can also freeze your tonics in ice cube trays. Once frozen, you can store the tonic ice cubes in a freezer-safe bag for up to two months. The average ice cube is 1 fluid ounce (30 ml), so a single shot serving would be two ice cubes. There are many different-sized ice cube trays now, so you could freeze your shots in various serving sizes. Label the storage bag with the name of the tonic and the use-by date. Defrost the ice cubes in a covered container in the refrigerator and consume within four days. A microwave is also good for defrosting.

Lastly, cleaning your equipment immediately is imperative. Your blender, juicer, and other equipment should also be cleaned as soon as possible after using to avoid pathogenic bacteria from growing.

Taking Your Tonic

The portion size of the vast majority of the shots is a ¼ cup / 2 ounces (60 ml). Taking one shot each day for just a few days can help add some nutrients to your diet, but your best results will be to continue to take the tonic regularly. You can even rotate among several tonics. That way you will get a greater variety of nutrients. If you don't consume enough of a specific nutrient, drinking a tonic that features that nutrient daily over weeks and months can help provide the body more of it. Just remember, more isn't better, so stick to the recommended portions per day.

When you take your tonic is up to you. You can take it when you wake up in the morning, with a meal or snack anytime during the day, or before bed. You can even take it with every meal—one serving up to three times a day. One or two servings of a tonic is typically not a lot of calories, and the typical ¼-cup (60 ml) portion does help add nutrients to your body. You can easily double or triple the serving to ½ or ¾ cup (125 or 175 ml) and drink it once a day.

A healthy eating plan works hand-in-hand with health shots. To visualize a healthy meal, picture half your plate filled with fruits and/or vegetables, a quarter of your plate with lean protein, and a quarter with starches, with at least half being whole grains. To further balance things out, add a serving of a low-fat or nonfat dairy or soy milk or soy yogurt, and a healthy fat. An example of these elements coming together on a plate would be: 5 ounces (140 g) of baked salmon on a quarter of the plate, roasted cauliflower and broccoli on half of the plate, and farro with mushrooms and cheese and a slice of avocado on the remaining quarter of the plate.

Basic Tonic Techniques

There are four basic tonic techniques used in this cookbook: juiced, blended, steeped, and shaken. Some recipes use a combination of these methods. At the start of each recipe you will find the method or methods it uses. Below you will find an overview of each method:

JUICED • In order to juice fruits, vegetables, and herbs, you will need an electric juicer. This appliance separates the juice from the rest of the fruit or vegetable, leaving the pulp, seeds, and skin to be discarded. You can typically juice produce with the skin on; if you do need to peel the skin, it is noted in the recipe.

BLENDED • A blender is needed to process the ingredients into a drinkable form. Typically, all the ingredients can be added together to make the tonic, but there are some recipes in which ingredients are added in a certain order, so do read each recipe carefully before beginning.

STEEPED • A small saucepan is best for heating and steeping ingredients, and a lid is required for some recipes. The heated ingredients are then cooled, if necessary, and strained through a sieve or strainer into a small bowl. You'll discard the solids and drink the tonic.

SHAKEN • Some tonics do not require cooking or heating. Ingredients are shaken in a glass jar with a tight-fitting lid or whisked in a bowl. The result is a quick tonic that can be served right away or chilled in the refrigerator before serving.

You will also notice that some recipes suggest serving the tonic warm or cold. Contrary to popular belief, temperature does not influence the way the tonic works in your body, because your body is designed to regulate the temperature internally. Sometimes, it just feels good to have a warm tonic, or conversely, sometimes you just want a cool, refreshing beverage.

Each of the following eight chapters focuses on a health issue and begins with an explanation of the issue and the ingredients in the recipes that are linked to addressing that health condition. Now that you know how it works, review the health conditions in the book and select the recipes you'd like to try. I wish you a delicious journey into the world of health shots!

Toby

Chapter 2

Immunity Shots

RECIPES

Immunity Overview

Keeping your immune system in tip-top shape is the first line of defense to safeguarding your health. If the immune system is healthy, it is easier to fight bacteria, viruses, or any other pathogen trying to make your body sick. Unhealthy eating, a lack of fruits and vegetables, insufficient fluids, a lack of regular exercise, excess stress, and drinking more than a moderate amount of alcohol can all negatively affect your immune system.

A healthy, balanced diet filled with whole grains, fruits, vegetables, healthy fats, nuts, seeds, lean protein, and low-fat and nonfat milk and other dairy foods is always your best bet for an efficient immune system. The tonics in this chapter help ensure consumption of specific nutrients that can build your immunity to its peak potential.

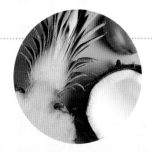

Below is a list of top nutrients that can help boost immunity and some of the foods and beverages in which they are found.

BROMELAIN • pineapple

CAPSAICIN • cayenne pepper

COPPER • mushrooms

CURCUMIN • turmeric

GINGEROL • ginger

IODINE • Greek yogurt

IRON • spinach

POTASSIUM • coconut water

RESVERATROL • grapes

SELENIUM • oats

VITAMIN A • Greek yogurt

VITAMIN C • kiwis, celery, lemons, limes, pears, oranges, pineapple

VITAMIN E • almond milk, peach nectar

ZINC • oats, mushrooms

Green Immunity Shots

Your juicer is a wonderful tool for creating delicious, nutrient-filled tonics. This tonic made from green fruits and veggies is filled with antioxidants and veggie water to help fight free radicals and aid in keeping you hydrated.

RECIPE TYPE
- juiced

HEAVY-HITTING NUTRIENTS
- iron, vitamin C

Makes 1½ cups (350 ml) or 6 shots
One shot: ¼ cup (60 ml)

- 2 Kirby or mini cucumbers, cut into large chunks
- 2 celery ribs, trimmed and cut into chunks
- 1 cup (30 g) baby spinach leaves
- 1 kiwi, cut in half
- ½ Granny Smith apple, cut in half

Place the cucumbers, celery, spinach, kiwi, and apple in a juicer and juice. Pour up to 3 shots into a glass and serve.

To store, pour into an airtight container, cover, and place in the refrigerator for up to 4 days. Alternatively, pour shots into ice cube trays, cover or store in a freezer bag, and freeze for up to 2 months. Always label and date your tonics.

Tonic Tip Cover and store the remaining apple for up to 5 days in the refrigerator to make this tonic again.

Vitamin C Protector Shots

Citrus fruits like lemons and limes are packed with the antioxidant vitamin C, which helps rid the body of free radicals that cause damage to your cells. You can whip up this tonic in just a few minutes by using a lemon squeezer or reamer, which means no juicer needed and less clean up.

RECIPE TYPE
- shaken

HEAVY-HITTING NUTRIENTS
- vitamin C

Makes 1 cup (250 ml) or 4 shots
One shot: ¼ cup (60 ml)

- ¾ cup (175 ml) water
- 2 tablespoons (30 ml) freshly squeezed lemon juice
- 2 tablespoons (30 ml) freshly squeezed lime juice
- 1 teaspoon (5 ml) honey
- 4 fresh mint leaves

1. Combine the water, lemon juice, lime juice, and honey in a small bowl and whisk to combine.

2. Pour up to 2 shots into a glass, garnish with 1 to 2 mint leaves, and serve. Or cover and chill in the refrigerator for up to 2 hours for a refreshing drink.

To store, pour into an airtight container, cover, and place in the refrigerator for up to 4 days. Alternatively, pour shots into ice cube trays, cover or store in a freezer bag, and freeze for up to 2 months. Always label and date your tonics.

 If you purchased extra mint, try it in the Dark Chocolate Mind Sharpener (page 46).

Immune System– Supporting Oat Blend

Oats provide fiber and an array of nutrients that help keep your immune system working properly, including zinc, iron, copper, and selenium. Once you allow the oats to soak up the goodness of the nectar, they blend beautifully into a refreshing tonic.

RECIPE TYPE
* blended

HEAVY-HITTING NUTRIENTS
* iodine, iron, selenium, vitamin A, vitamin E, zinc

Makes 1 cup (250 ml) or 4 shots
One shot: ¼ cup (60 ml)

* ½ cup (125 ml) unsweetened almond milk
* ¼ cup (25 g) old-fashioned rolled oats
* ¼ teaspoon (1 g) ground cinnamon
* 2 tablespoons (30 ml) plain nonfat Greek yogurt
* ½ cup (125 ml) peach nectar (see Tip)

1. Place the almond milk, oats, and cinnamon in the blender and stir with a spoon to combine (don't turn on the blender yet). Allow the mixture to sit for 15 minutes, or until the liquid is absorbed.

2. Add the yogurt and nectar to the blender and blend on high for 1 minute, or until smooth. Pour up to 2 shots into a glass and serve.

3. Store as you would all cold health shots.

Tonic Tip Mix leftover peach nectar in lemonade, smoothies, or the Spiced Pear Immunity Booster (page 23).

Zesty Immune System-Defending Tonic

This warming tonic is a combination of numerous powerful antioxidants and anti-inflammatory compounds. The cayenne pepper gives it a mild but tasty kick.

RECIPE TYPE
* steeped

HEAVY-HITTING NUTRIENTS
* capsaicin, curcumin, gingerol, vitamin C

Makes 1 cup (250 ml) or 4 shots
One shot: ¼ cup (60 ml)

* 1 lemon
* 1¼ cups (300 ml) water
* 1-inch (2.5 cm) piece fresh ginger, cut into chunks
* 2 teaspoons (10 ml) pure maple syrup
* ¼ teaspoon (1 g) ground turmeric
* ⅛ teaspoon (0.5 g) cayenne pepper (see Tip)

1. Remove 4 long strips of peel from the lemon and set aside. Juice the lemon to get at least 2 tablespoons (30 ml).

2. Stir together the water, lemon juice and peel, ginger, maple syrup, turmeric, and cayenne in a small saucepan and bring to a boil over high heat. Reduce the heat to medium-low and simmer, stirring occasionally, for 15 minutes to allow flavors to combine. Remove pan from the heat and allow to cool for 10 minutes.

3. Remove and discard the solids. Pour up to 2 shots into a small mug or heatproof glass and serve warm.

To store, cool, then pour into an airtight container, cover, and place in the refrigerator for up to 4 days. Alternatively, pour shots into ice cube trays, cover or store in a freezer bag, and freeze for up to 2 months. Always label and date your tonics.

To reheat, place a shot, defrosted if necessary, in a small saucepan and bring to a boil over high heat, stirring occasionally. Remove pan from the heat and allow tonic to cool slightly. Pour into a small mug or heatproof glass and serve.

 To add more spice, use ¼ teaspoon (1 g) cayenne pepper.

Spiced Pear Immunity Booster

This shot helps get your immune system in tip-top shape by simmering flavorful fresh thyme and ginger with orange peel, which is valuable for its oils and nutrients. The pear juice or pear nectar are available in the juice section of most grocery stores. Enjoy this tonic warm or at room temperature.

RECIPE TYPE
* steeped

HEAVY-HITTING NUTRIENTS
* gingerol, vitamin C

Makes 1½ cups (350 ml) or 6 shots
One shot: ¼ cup (60 ml)

* 1 cup (250 ml) water
* 1-inch (2.5 cm) piece fresh ginger, thinly sliced
* 6 sprigs fresh thyme
* Four 1-inch (2.5 cm) strips orange peel
* ½ cup (125 ml) pear nectar or pure pear juice

1. Combine the water, ginger, thyme, and orange peel in a small saucepan and bring to a boil over high heat. Remove pan from the heat and allow to steep, covered, for 15 minutes.

2. Strain the liquid into a bowl and discard the solids. Stir in the pear nectar until combined. Pour up to 3 shots into a glass and serve warm or at room temperature.

(recipe continues)

To store, cool, then pour into an airtight container, cover, and place in the refrigerator for up to 4 days. Alternatively, pour shots into ice cube trays, cover or store in a freezer bag, and freeze for up to 2 months. Always label and date your tonics.

Tonic Tip

If you purchased a large bunch of thyme, use the extra to blend into a smoothie or whisk into a salad dressing.

Nectar is thicker than juice as it tends to be pureed fruit. It is then diluted with water to thin it out to a drinkable consistency. Nectar tends to have some additives to help preserve the flavor and shelf life.

Immune System–Balancing Mushroom Shots

Dried mushrooms have a savory, umami flavor and provide an array of nutrients to help keep your immune system strong. Store extra dried mushrooms in your pantry so you always have them on hand to whip up this tonic.

RECIPE TYPE
- steeped

HEAVY-HITTING NUTRIENTS
- bromelain, copper, vitamin C, zinc

Makes 1½ cups (350 ml) or 6 shots
One shot: ¼ cup (60 ml)

- 1 lemon
- 1⅓ cups (325 ml) water
- ½ cup (8 g) dried shiitake mushrooms
- ¼ cup (60 ml) 100% pineapple juice

1. Remove 3 to 4 strips of peel from the lemon and set aside. Juice the lemon to get at least 2 tablespoons (30 ml).

2. Bring the water to a boil in a small saucepan over high heat. Remove pan from the heat and add the lemon juice and peel, mushrooms, and pineapple juice; stir to combine. Allow mixture to stand, covered, for 1 hour.

3. Strain the liquid into a bowl and discard solids. Pour up to 3 shots into a glass and serve warm or at room temperature.

(recipe continues)

To store, cool, then pour into an airtight container, cover, and place in the refrigerator for up to 4 days. Alternatively, pour shots into ice cube trays, cover or store in a freezer bag, and freeze for up to 2 months. Always label and date your tonics.

To reheat, pour the shot, defrosted if necessary, into a small saucepan and bring to a boil over high heat, stirring occasionally. Remove pan from the heat and allow tonic to cool slightly. Pour into a small mug or heatproof glass and serve.

 Store dried shiitake mushrooms in an airtight container in a cool, dry place for up to 6 months.

Pathogen–Fighting Grape Tonic

Grapes contain a natural compound called resveratrol that helps fight pathogenic bacteria. The lime will load you up with antioxidant vitamin C. It's a powerful combo!

RECIPE TYPE
- blended

HEAVY-HITTING NUTRIENTS
- potassium, resveratrol, vitamin C

Makes 1½ cups (350 ml) or 6 shots
One shot: ¼ cup (60 ml)

- 1 cup (140 g) seedless green or red grapes
- 1 cup (30 g) baby spinach leaves
- ½ cup (125 ml) coconut water
- Juice of 1 lime

Place the grapes, spinach, coconut water, and lime juice in a blender and blend on high for 1 minute until smooth. Pour up to 3 shots into a glass and serve.

To store, pour into an airtight container, cover, and place in the refrigerator for up to 4 days. Alternatively, pour shots into ice cube trays, cover or store in a freezer bag, and freeze for up to 2 months. Always label and date your tonics.

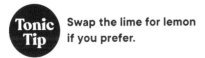 **Swap the lime for lemon if you prefer.**

Chapter 3

Anti-Inflammatory Shots

Anti-Inflammatory Overview

Inflammation is your body's way of defending against foreign invaders. It also helps you heal from injury. However, inflammation can become chronic, which can interrupt and damage your body's cells. Cell damage can contribute to the development of chronic diseases such as heart disease, type 2 diabetes, arthritis, and certain forms of cancer.

Foods high in added sugar, saturated fat, and trans fat can contribute to inflammation. Consuming too much alcohol—more than the recommended one to two drinks per day for women and men, respectively—can also lead to inflammation. The tonics in this chapter can help boost the nutrients your body uses to fight inflammation.

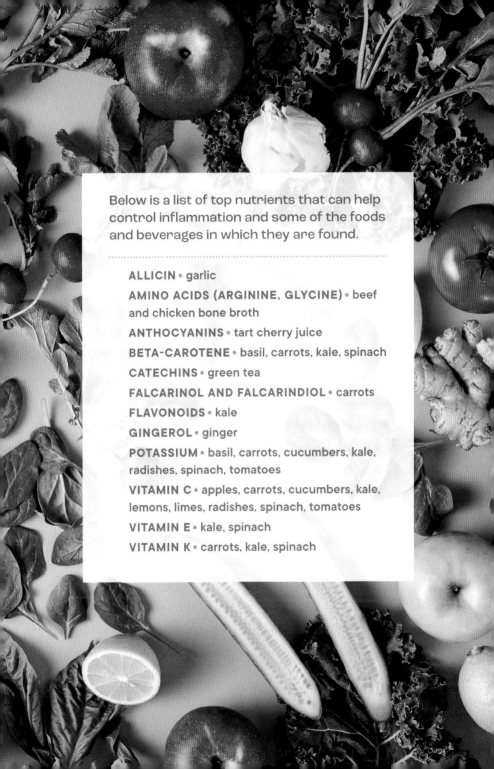

Below is a list of top nutrients that can help control inflammation and some of the foods and beverages in which they are found.

ALLICIN • garlic

AMINO ACIDS (ARGININE, GLYCINE) • beef and chicken bone broth

ANTHOCYANINS • tart cherry juice

BETA-CAROTENE • basil, carrots, kale, spinach

CATECHINS • green tea

FALCARINOL AND FALCARINDIOL • carrots

FLAVONOIDS • kale

GINGEROL • ginger

POTASSIUM • basil, carrots, cucumbers, kale, radishes, spinach, tomatoes

VITAMIN C • apples, carrots, cucumbers, kale, lemons, limes, radishes, spinach, tomatoes

VITAMIN E • kale, spinach

VITAMIN K • carrots, kale, spinach

Antioxidant Tomato Tonic

Tomatoes have a boatload of the antioxidant vitamin C, while carrots are brimming with beta-carotene, which is the antioxidant that your body converts to vitamin A. You'll also get a slight spicy punch and some additional vitamin C from the radishes.

RECIPE TYPE
- juiced

HEAVY-HITTING NUTRIENTS
- beta-carotene, potassium, vitamin C

Makes 1 cup (250 ml) or 4 shots
One shot: ¼ cup (60 ml)

- 2 medium carrots, cut into large chunks
- 2 radishes
- 2 medium plum tomatoes, quartered
- 1 Kirby or mini cucumber, cut into large chunks
- ¼ cup (8 g) fresh basil leaves

Place the carrots, radishes, tomatoes, cucumber, and basil in a juicer and juice. Pour up to 2 shots into a glass and serve.

To store, pour into an airtight container, cover, and place in the refrigerator for up to 4 days. Alternatively, pour shots into ice cube trays, cover or store in a freezer bag, and freeze for up to 2 months. Always label and date your tonics.

 For more spice, add an additional radish.

Spiced Green Tea Tonic

Green tea contains natural compounds called catechins that can help decrease inflammation. Ginger and honey also have anti-inflammatory compounds in them. This is a delicious trio of foods providing anti-inflammatory benefits.

RECIPE TYPE
- steeped

HEAVY-HITTING NUTRIENTS
- catechins, gingerol

Makes 1 cup (250 ml) or 4 shots
One shot: ¼ cup (60 ml)

- 1 green tea bag
- 1 cup (250 ml) boiling water
- 1 teaspoon (5 ml) honey
- ⅛ teaspoon (0.5 g) ground ginger

1. Place the tea bag in a mug filled with boiling water and steep for exactly 3 minutes (any longer makes it bitter). Remove the tea bag and discard. Stir in the honey and ginger. Allow to cool for 5 minutes.

2. Pour up to 2 shots into a small mug or heatproof glass and serve warm.

To store, cool, then pour into an airtight container, cover, and place in the refrigerator for up to 4 days. Alternatively, pour shots into ice cube trays, cover or store in a freezer bag, and freeze for up to 2 months. Always label and date your tonics.

To reheat, pour the shot into a small saucepan, defrosted if necessary, and bring to a boil over high heat, stirring occasionally. Remove pan from the heat and allow tonic to cool slightly. Pour into a small mug or heatproof glass and serve.

Orange Inflammation–Fighter Shots

Enjoy these sweet, slightly spicy shots that provide inflammation-stomping vitamin A from the carrots—which also have two additional anti-inflammation compounds called falcarinol and falcarindiol. It's a powerful combo!

RECIPE TYPE
- juiced then shaken

HEAVY-HITTING NUTRIENTS
- beta-carotene, falcarinol, falcarindiol, gingerol, vitamin K

Makes 1½ cups (350 ml) or 6 shots
One shot: ¼ cup (60 ml)

- 4 medium carrots, cut into large chunks
- 2-inch (5 cm) piece fresh ginger
- ¾ cup (175 ml) coconut water
- ⅛ teaspoon (0.5 g) sea salt
- Pinch of ground black pepper

1. Place the carrots and ginger in a juicer and juice.

2. Combine the juice, coconut water, salt, and pepper in a container with a tight-fitting lid. Cover and shake for about 15 seconds, or until well combined. Pour up to 3 shots into a glass and serve.

3. Store as you would all cold health shots.

 Tonic Tip Store whole, unpeeled carrots wrapped in a paper towel and in an airtight container in the coolest part of the refrigerator. Do not rinse before storing.

Warm Inflammation- Reducing Shots

Bone broth contains collagen, which holds several amino acids that help reduce inflammation. There are many healthy packaged brands of bone broth you can pick up at your local market. Choose beef or chicken bone broth options that are reduced or no-added-sodium versions.

RECIPE TYPE
- steeped

HEAVY-HITTING NUTRIENTS
- allicin, arginine, glycine, vitamin C

Makes 1 cup (250 ml) or 4 shots
One shot: ¼ cup (60 ml)

- 1 lemon
- 1¼ cups (300 ml) chicken bone broth or beef bone broth
- 1 medium scallion, green and white parts roughly sliced
- 1 clove garlic, thinly sliced
- 5 black peppercorns

1. Remove 3 or 4 strips of peel from the lemon and set aside.

2. Combine the lemon peel, bone broth, scallion, garlic, and peppercorns in a small saucepan and bring to a boil over high heat. Remove pan from the heat and steep, covered, for 15 minutes.

3. Strain the liquid into a bowl and discard the solids. Pour up to 2 shots into a small mug or heatproof glass and serve warm.

To store, cool, then pour into an airtight container, cover, and place in

(recipe continues)

the refrigerator for up to 4 days. Alternatively, pour shots into ice cube trays, cover or store in a freezer bag, and freeze for up to 2 months. Always label and date your tonics.

To reheat, pour the shot, defrosted if necessary, into a small saucepan and bring to a boil over high heat, stirring occasionally. Remove pan from the heat and allow tonic to cool slightly. Pour into a small mug or heatproof glass and serve.

 If you like your tonic with a stronger lemon flavor, add more lemon peel.

Inflammation-Suppressing Vitamin K Shots

Vitamin K, great for your bones and blood, is found in green leafy vegetables like kale and spinach. These power veggies also provide vitamin C and flavonoids to help decrease inflammation. The green apple adds a sweet-tart flavor, as well as more vitamin C.

RECIPE TYPE
- juiced

HEAVY-HITTING NUTRIENTS
- flavonoids, vitamin C, vitamin E, vitamin K

Makes 1½ cups (350 ml) or 6 shots
One shot: ¼ cup (60 ml)

- 2 Kirby or mini cucumbers, cut into chunks
- 1 Granny Smith apple, quartered
- 1 cup (20 g) chopped kale leaves
- 1 cup (30 g) baby spinach leaves

Place the cucumber, apple, kale, and spinach in a juicer and juice. Pour up to 3 shots into a glass and serve.

To store, pour into an airtight container, cover, and place in the refrigerator for up to 4 days. Alternatively, pour shots into ice cube trays, cover or store in a freezer bag, and freeze for up to 2 months. Always label and date your tonics.

Tonic Tip Swap the Kirby cucumbers for 1 small cucumber or a third of an English cucumber.

Tart Cherry Tonic

Tart cherry juice is made from Montmorency cherries, also known as sour cherries. They are brimming with antioxidants, including anthocyanins, which have been shown to help decrease inflammation.

RECIPE TYPE
- shaken

HEAVY-HITTING NUTRIENTS
- anthocyanins, gingerol, vitamin C

Makes 1 cup (250 ml) or 4 shots
One shot: ¼ cup (60 ml)

- 1 cup (250 ml) no-sugar-added 100% tart cherry juice
- Juice of 1 lime
- ⅛ teaspoon (0.5 g) ground ginger

1. Place the cherry juice, lime juice, and ginger in a small jar and close tightly. Shake for 30 seconds until well combined. Pour up to 2 shots into a glass and serve.

2. To serve cold, cover the jar and place in the refrigerate to chill for up to 2 hours.

To store, pour into airtight container, cover, and place in the refrigerator for up to 4 days. Alternatively, pour shots into ice cube trays, cover or store in a freezer bag, and freeze for up to 2 months. Always label and date your tonics.

 Tonic Tip You can find tart cherry juice in the juice aisle; be sure it says "tart" and "no-sugar-added" on the label.

Chapter 4

Brain Health Shots

RECIPES

Brain Health Overview

What you eat affects your body *and* your brain. Although there is no one specific food that will prevent cognitive decline, eating a healthy, well-balanced diet can help support brain health including memory and concentration. As it turns out, many of these foods are good for heart health, too.

To help keep mentally sharp, avoid foods that can negatively impact cognitive function, such as foods high in trans fat, saturated fat, added sugar; as well as consuming too much alcohol.

To promote cognitive health and overall brain function, the MIND diet was created. It combines food and lifestyle recommendations from the Mediterranean and DASH diets. The tonic recipes in this chapter feature many of the foods from the MIND diet.

Below is a list of top nutrients that have been linked to supporting brain health and some of the foods and beverages in which they are found.

ANTHOCYANINS • blueberries, pomegranate juice, strawberries, tart cherry juice

BETA-CAROTENE • kale, tart cherry juice

CINNAMALDEHYDE • cinnamon

FLAVANOLS • unsweetened cocoa powder

FOLATE • oranges, rosemary

HESPERIDIN • oranges

VITAMIN C • apples, blueberries, cardamom, celery, cucumbers, lemons, mint, oranges, pomegranate juice, strawberries, tart cherry juice

Dark Chocolate Mind Sharpener

Some of the compounds linked to improving memory and cognitive health include flavanols, found in unsweetened cocoa powder, protein in milk, and cinnamaldehyde, found in cinnamon. This rich tonic is similar to warm cocoa. Mmmmm.

RECIPE TYPE
- steeped

HEAVY-HITTING NUTRIENTS
- cinnamaldehyde, flavanols

Makes 1½ cups (350 ml) or 6 shots
One shot: ¼ cup (60 ml)

- 1¾ cups (425 ml) whole milk
- 1 tablespoon (5 g) unsweetened cocoa powder
- 2 teaspoons (10 ml) honey
- ⅛ teaspoon (0.5 g) ground cinnamon
- ⅛ teaspoon (0.5 g) ground cardamom
- 6 fresh mint leaves

1. Heat the milk over medium-high heat in a medium saucepan, whisking regularly until it just begins to boil. Whisk in the cocoa powder, honey, cinnamon, and cardamom until incorporated.

2. Remove pan from the heat and stir in the mint leaves. Set the pan aside for 5 minutes to allow the flavors to blend.

3. Remove the mint leaves and discard. Pour up to 3 shots into a small mug or heatproof glass and serve warm.

To store, cool, then pour into an airtight container, cover, and place in the refrigerator for up to 4 days. Alternatively, pour shots into ice cube trays, cover or store in a freezer bag, and freeze for up to 2 months. Always label and date your tonics.

To reheat, pour the shot into a small saucepan, defrosting if necessary, and bring to a simmer over medium heat, whisking regularly. Remove pan from the heat and allow tonic to cool slightly. Pour into a small mug or heatproof glass and serve.

Whisking the milk regularly will ensure your tonic remains nice and creamy.

Brain-Protecting Orange-Cardamom Tonic

Many nutrients found in orange juice help protect cognitive function. Here, the OJ is paired with cardamom, which provides folate and vitamin C to help brain function. If you want even more of these natural nutrients, double your shot!

RECIPE TYPE
- steeped

HEAVY-HITTING NUTRIENTS
- folate, hesperidin, vitamin C

Makes 1 cup (250 ml) or 4 shots
One shot: ¼ cup (60 ml)

- 1¼ cups (300 ml) freshly squeezed orange juice (from about 4 navel oranges)
- 4 whole cardamom pods

1. Place the orange juice and cardamom in a small saucepan and bring to a boil over high heat. Reduce the heat to low and simmer, covered, for 10 minutes. Set the pan aside to cool slightly for 5 minutes.

2. Strain the liquid into a bowl and discard the solids. Pour the mixture into a container, cover, and chill. Once cold, pour up to 2 shots into a glass and enjoy.

To store, cool, then pour into an airtight container, cover, and place in the refrigerator for up to 4 days. Alternatively, pour shots into ice cube trays, cover or store in a freezer bag, and freeze for up to 2 months. Always label and date your tonics.

Tonic Tip Swap the whole cardamom pods for ⅛ teaspoon (0.5 g) of ground cardamom.

Beta-Carotene Brain Tonic

The antioxidants beta-carotene and vitamin C help protect against oxidative stress to help keep your brain healthy. You will find both of these powerful nutrients in this naturally sweet tonic.

RECIPE TYPE
- juicing

HEAVY-HITTING NUTRIENTS
- beta-carotene, vitamin C

Makes 1½ cups (350 ml) or 6 shots
One shot: ¼ cup (60 ml)

- 2 Kirby or mini cucumbers, cut into large chunks
- 2 ribs celery, cut into large chunks
- 1 Granny Smith apple, quartered
- 1 cup (20 g) chopped kale
- ½ lemon

Place the cucumbers, celery, apple, kale, and lemon in a juicer and juice. Pour up to 3 shots into a glass and serve.

To store, pour into an airtight container, cover, and place in the refrigerator for up to 4 days. Alternatively, pour shots into ice cube trays, cover or store in a freezer bag, and freeze for up to 2 months. Always label and date your tonics.

Peel the lemon before juicing and save the rind to use in other tonic recipes such as the Pomegranate-Cinnamon Brain Shots (page 56).

Mixed-Berry Brain Booster

Anthocyanins are natural plant compounds that give berries their beautiful red, blue, or purple hue. These compounds have been found to have a brain-protective role due to their anti-inflammatory and antioxidant properties. Enjoy this berry blend with a smoothie consistency—it has a slightly larger portion size than other recipes and even more nutrients.

RECIPE TYPE
* blended

HEAVY-HITTING NUTRIENTS
* anthocyanins, hespiridin

Makes 2 cups (500 ml) or 8 shots
One shot: ½ cup (125 ml)

* 1 cup (150 g) frozen strawberries
* 1 cup (155 g) frozen blueberries
* 1 cup (250 ml) 100% orange juice
* ½ cup (125 ml) plain low-fat Greek yogurt

Place the strawberries, blueberries, orange juice, and yogurt in a blender and blend on high for 1 minute, or until smooth. Pour up to 2 shots into a glass and serve immediately.

I don't recommend storing this tonic. The texture changes pretty quickly and it's not as good, so halve or quarter the recipe to serve up to 2 shots.

Swap in blackberries or raspberries for either of the berries.

Rosemary–Lemon Memory Enhancing Shots

Lemons are brimming with the antioxidant vitamin C, which helps protect brain cells. Research suggests that low levels of vitamin C may be linked to an impaired ability to think and remember. With it's sweet-tart flavor and nourishing ingredients, this shot will get you on your way!

RECIPE TYPE
• shaken

HEAVY-HITTING NUTRIENTS
• folate, vitamin C

Makes 1 cup (250 ml) or 4 shots
One shot: ¼ cup (60 ml)

- Juice of 3 lemons
- ½ cup (125 ml) water
- 2 teaspoons (10 ml) honey
- 2 sprigs fresh rosemary
- 3 fresh mint leaves

1. In a medium bowl, whisk together the lemon juice, water, and honey. Add the rosemary sprigs and mint leaves and stir to combine.

2. Cover and place in the refrigerator to chill and allow the flavors to combine for 1 to 2 hours. Strain and discard the solids.

3. Shake vigorously, then pour up to 2 shots into a glass and serve warm.

4. Store as you would all cold health shots.

Tonic Tip Swap the lemon juice for the juice of 2 navel oranges or 1 pink grapefruit.

Clarifying Blueberry Tonic

Wild blueberries and tart cherry juice provide anthocyanins, which may help improve brain performance. This delicious blend is tart, with notes that are both sweet and a bit savory, making it a deliciously healthy tonic.

RECIPE TYPE
• steeped then blended

HEAVY-HITTING NUTRIENTS
• anthocyanins, vitamin C

Makes 1 cup (250 ml) or 4 shots
One shot: ¼ cup (60 ml)

- 1 cup (155 g) frozen wild blueberries
- ½ cup (125 ml) no-sugar-added 100% tart cherry juice, divided
- 1 teaspoon (5 ml) pure maple syrup
- 4 basil leaves
- ⅓ cup (75 ml) cold water

1. Combine the blueberries, ¼ cup (60 ml) cherry juice, maple syrup, and basil leaves in a small saucepan and bring to a boil over high heat. Reduce the heat to medium-low and simmer, stirring occasionally, until the blueberries burst and turn gel-like, about 20 minutes. Set the pan aside and allow to cool for at least 10 minutes.

2. Combine the blueberry mixture, water, and remaining ¼ cup (60 ml) cherry juice in a blender and blend on high for 30 seconds or until smooth.

3. Pour up to 2 shots into a heatproof glass or mug and serve warm or at room temperature.

(recipe continues)

To store, cool, then pour into an airtight container, cover, and place in the refrigerator for up to 4 days. Alternatively, pour shots into ice cube trays, cover or store in a freezer bag, and freeze for up to 2 months. Always label and date your tonics.

 Wild blueberries are found in the frozen fruit aisle. They are smaller and slightly sweeter than ordinary blueberries and also provide 33% more anthocyanins.

Pomegranate–Cinnamon Brain Shots

Your home will be filled with the scent of delicious warming spices as this tonic cooks in your kitchen. Then enjoy the flavors as they provide goodness to your body—specifically to your brain.

RECIPE TYPE
- steeped

HEAVY-HITTING NUTRIENTS
- anthocyanins, vitamin C

Makes 1½ cups (350 ml) or 6 shots
One shot: ¼ cup (60 ml)

- 1¾ cups (425 ml) 100% pomegranate juice
- 1 teaspoon (5 ml) vanilla extract
- Four 2-inch (5 cm) strips lemon peel
- 3 cinnamon sticks
- 3 cardamom pods
- 3 whole cloves
- 3 whole allspice berries

1. Combine the pomegranate juice, vanilla, lemon peel, cinnamon, cardamom, cloves, and allspice in a small saucepan and bring to a boil over high heat. Reduce the heat to medium-low and simmer, covered, for about 20 minutes to allow the flavors to combine. Remove pan from heat and allow to cool for 10 minutes.

2. Strain the liquid into a bowl and discard the solids. Pour up to 3 shots into a small mug or heatproof glass and serve warm.

To store, cool, then pour into an airtight container, cover, and place in the refrigerator for up to 4 days. Alternatively, pour shots into ice cube trays, cover or store in a freezer bag, and freeze for up to 2 months. Always label and date your tonics.

To reheat, pour the shot, defrosted if necessary, into a small saucepan and bring to a boil over high heat, whisking regularly. Remove pan from the heat and allow tonic to cool slightly. Pour into a small mug or heatproof glass and serve.

 This is a great drink to share with friends. Double or triple the batch and serve in mugs with cinnamon sticks.

Chapter 5

Sleep Shots

RECIPES

Sleep Overview

Sleep is vital for physical and mental recharging. Major physical and psychological events occur in your body when you sleep, including adjustments of hormone levels, muscle repair, processing memories, and general rejuvenation.

Your main hunger-control hormones, leptin and ghrelin, need sleep to function. If you're not sleeping, these hormones can get thrown off track and result in strong feelings of hunger that can lead to overeating. Sleep also allows for muscle and tissue repair by keeping your body still during a good overnight slumber. Lack of sleep can end up putting stress on this repair system, impacting your overall muscle health. Lastly, inadequate sleep can trigger behavioral effects, including lapsing attention, memory issues, and depressed mood. A psychological behavioral response from not getting enough zzz's can be seen when you wake up cranky and irritable. Try the following tonics to help relax your body and mind to get a good night's sleep.

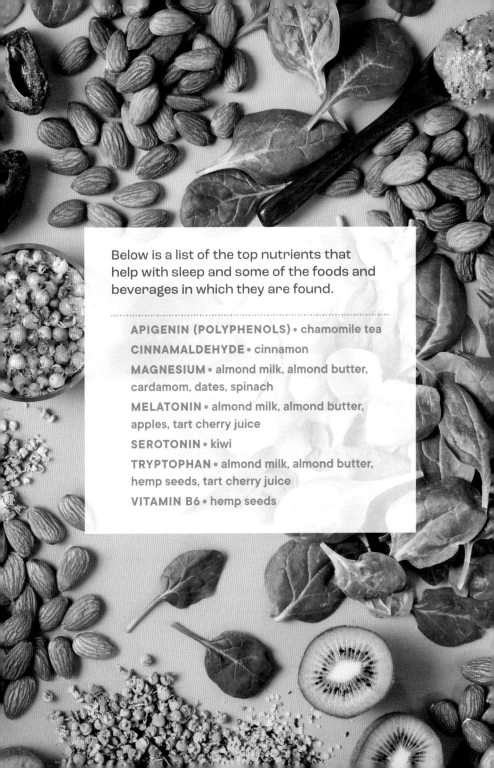

Below is a list of the top nutrients that help with sleep and some of the foods and beverages in which they are found.

....

APIGENIN (POLYPHENOLS) • chamomile tea

CINNAMALDEHYDE • cinnamon

MAGNESIUM • almond milk, almond butter, cardamom, dates, spinach

MELATONIN • almond milk, almond butter, apples, tart cherry juice

SEROTONIN • kiwi

TRYPTOPHAN • almond milk, almond butter, hemp seeds, tart cherry juice

VITAMIN B6 • hemp seeds

Moon Milk Tonic

It may be more impression than science that says warm milk makes you sleepy, but if you mix that warm milk with hemp seeds and several spices, you get a tonic that contains natural plant compounds that can help you get your zzz's.

RECIPE TYPE
- steeped

HEAVY-HITTING NUTRIENTS
- cinnamaldehyde, tryptophan, vitamin B6

Makes 1½ cups (350 ml) or 6 shots
One shot: ¼ cup (60 ml)

- 1½ cups (350 ml) reduced-fat milk or unflavored soy milk
- 1 tablespoon (15 ml) pure maple syrup
- 2 teaspoons (5 g) ground hemp seeds
- ½ teaspoon (2 ml) vanilla extract
- ½ teaspoon (2 g) ground cinnamon
- ⅛ teaspoon (0.5 g) ground cardamom
- ⅛ teaspoon (0.5 g) ground nutmeg

1. Combine the milk, maple syrup, hemp seeds, vanilla, cinnamon, cardamom, and nutmeg in a small saucepan and bring to a boil over high heat, whisking constantly. Reduce the heat to medium-low and simmer, uncovered, whisking constantly to allow the flavors to combine, about 3 minutes. Set the pan aside to cool slightly.

2. Pour up to 3 shots into a small mug or heatproof glass and serve warm.

To store, cool, then pour into an airtight container, cover, and place in the refrigerator for up to 4 days. Alternatively, pour shots into ice cube trays, cover or store in a freezer bag, and freeze for up to 2 months. Always label and date your tonics.

To reheat, defrost if necessary, then pour the shot into a small saucepan and bring to a boil over high heat, whisking regularly. Remove pan from the heat and allow tonic to cool slightly. Pour into a small mug or heatproof glass and serve.

Swap the maple syrup for honey for a different taste. Ground hemp seeds are available in health-food stores, large grocery stores, and online.

Before–Bedtime Lavender Relaxation Shots

Lavender has been touted as an anxiety reducer, and less anxiety can mean better sleep! You can find culinary lavender in the spice section of specialty food markets. Combine the lavender with the other nutrients, and this tonic practically sings you to sleep.

RECIPE TYPE
- steeped

HEAVY-HITTING NUTRIENTS
- apigenin (polyphenols)

Makes 1½ cups (350 ml) or 6 shots
One shot: ¼ cup (60 ml)

- 1½ cups (350 ml) water
- 1 chamomile tea bag
- 1 teaspoon (5 ml) honey
- 6 fresh mint leaves
- ⅛ teaspoon (0.5 g) culinary lavender

1. In a small saucepan, bring the water to a boil over high heat. Remove pan from the heat and add the tea bag. Steep for exactly 4 minutes, then remove the tea bag and discard. Whisk in the honey and stir in the mint leaves and lavender. Cover and set pan aside for 5 minutes to allow flavors to blend.

2. Strain the liquid into a bowl and discard the solids. Pour up to 3 shots into a small mug or heatproof glass and serve warm.

To store, cool, then pour into an airtight container, cover, and place in the refrigerator for up to 4 days. Alternatively, pour shots into ice cube trays, cover or store in a freezer bag, and freeze for up to 2 months. Always label and date your tonics.

To reheat, pour the shot into a small saucepan and bring to a boil over high heat, stirring occasionally. Remove pan from the heat and allow tonic to cool slightly. Pour into a small mug or heatproof glass and serve.

Tonic Tip

To store fresh mint in the refrigerator, rinse and pat dry. Wrap mint leaves in a moistened paper towel and place in a resealable bag, but don't seal it.

Natural Melatonin Almond Tonic

Melatonin is a hormone that helps your body sleep properly. It is found naturally in almonds and dates. Enjoy the sweetness of this combination before bedtime.

RECIPE TYPE
- blended

HEAVY-HITTING NUTRIENTS
- magnesium, melatonin, tryptophan

Makes 1½ cups (350 ml) or 6 shots
One shot: ¼ cup (60 ml)

- 1¼ cups (300 ml) unsweetened almond milk
- 2 tablespoons (32 g) almond butter
- 4 pitted medjool dates
- ⅛ teaspoon (0.5 g) ground cardamom

Place the almond milk, almond butter, dates, and cardamom in a blender and blend on high for 1 minute until smooth. Pour up to 3 shots into a glass and serve.

To store extra shots, pour shots of the mixture into individual containers or the remaining mixture into one large container, cover, and place in the refrigerator for up to 4 days. Label and date the container.

 **Tonic Tip** To add sweetness, use vanilla almond milk.

Steady-Sleep Shots

This shot is made by juicing produce that contains a variety of nutrients to promote a sense of calm and relaxation—all designed to give you a good night's rest.

RECIPE TYPE
- juiced

HEAVY-HITTING NUTRIENTS
- magnesium, melatonin, serotonin

Makes 1 cup (250 ml) or 4 shots
One shot: ¼ cup (60 ml)

- 2 cups (60 g) baby spinach leaves
- 2 ribs celery, cut into chunks
- 2 kiwis, skin on, cut in half
- ½ Granny Smith apple, cut in half
- ½ cup (15 g) flat leaf or curly parsley
- 2-inch (5 cm) piece fresh ginger

Place the spinach, celery, kiwi, apple, parsley, and ginger in a juicer and juice. Pour up to 2 shots into a glass and serve.

To store, pour into an airtight container, cover, and place in the refrigerator for up to 4 days. Alternatively, pour shots into ice cube trays, cover or store in a freezer bag, and freeze for up to 2 months. Always label and date your tonics.

 **Tonic Tip** If you'd like, replace spinach with kale.

Cherry–Chamomile Sleep Shots

Many folks drink chamomile tea in the evening to help them relax. This shot goes further by adding ingredients like tart cherry juice and almond butter that help promote sleep and relaxation.

RECIPE TYPE
- steeped then blended

HEAVY-HITTING NUTRIENTS
- apigenin, magnesium, melatonin, tryptophan

Makes 1½ cups (350 ml) or 6 shots
One shot: ¼ cup (60 ml)

- 1 chamomile tea bag
- 1 cup (250 ml) boiling water
- ½ cup (125 ml) no-sugar-added 100% tart cherry juice
- 2 tablespoons (32 g) almond butter
- ¼ teaspoon (1 g) ground cinnamon

1. Place the tea bag in a mug and add the boiling water. Steep for exactly 4 minutes. Remove the tea bag and set the tea aside to cool slightly.
2. Place the tea, cherry juice, almond butter, and cinnamon in a blender and blend until smooth. Pour up to 3 shots into a small mug or heatproof glass and serve warm.

To store, cool, then pour into an airtight container, cover, and place in the refrigerator for up to 4 days. Alternatively, pour shots into ice cube trays, cover or store in a freezer bag, and freeze for up to 2 months. Always label and date your tonics.

To reheat, defrost if necessary, then pour the shot into a small saucepan and bring to a boil over high heat, stirring occasionally. Remove pan from the heat and allow tonic to cool slightly. Pour into a small mug or heatproof glass and serve.

For something just a little different, replace the cherry juice with 100% pomegranate juice.

Dreamy Pink Sleep Tonic

The mix of almond milk and tart cherry juice creates a gorgeous pink tonic. There are many nutrients in both ingredients that support hormone health to improve sleep.

RECIPE TYPE
- shaken

HEAVY-HITTING NUTRIENTS
- magnesium, melatonin, tryptophan

Makes 1½ cups (350 ml) or 6 shots
One shot: ¼ cup (60 ml)

- 1 cup (250 ml) unsweetened almond milk
- ½ cup (125 ml) no-sugar-added 100% tart cherry juice
- 2 teaspoons (10 ml) pure maple syrup
- ¼ teaspoon (1 g) ground cinnamon

Place the almond milk, cherry juice, maple syrup, and cinnamon in a container with a tight-fitting lid. Cover and shake for about 15 seconds, or until well combined. Pour up to 3 shots into a glass and serve.

To store, pour into an airtight container, cover, and place in the refrigerator for up to 4 days. Alternatively, pour shots into ice cube trays, cover or store in a freezer bag, and freeze for up to 2 months. Always label and date your tonics.

When buying maple syrup, purchase the real deal, ones labeled 100% maple syrup. The other kinds of "maple-type syrup" are filled with added sugar and have no beneficial nutrients.

Chapter 6

Gut Health Shots

Gut Health Overview

Your gut contains a microbiome, an environment where microorganisms live and interact with their surroundings within your digestive tract. When you keep your gut populated with healthy bacteria, it benefits your digestive health and your immune system. Foods with probiotics contain live microorganisms that help maintain or improve the healthy bacteria in your gut. Prebiotics feed your gut bacteria and are found in foods that are high in fiber. Both probiotics and prebiotics work hand in hand to help create a healthier microbiome.

Fiber also helps keep your gastrointestinal tract healthy. The recommended amount of fiber is between 28 to 40 grams per day, but most Americans consume less than half that. In addition to getting in some fiber in a tonic, aim to increase fiber intake by eating a varied diet with plenty of whole grains, nuts, seeds, beans, lentils, peas, fruits, and vegetables.

Below is a list of top nutrients that can help boost gut health and some of the foods and beverages in which they are found.

FIBER • apples, bananas, cucumbers, flaxseed, mango, pineapple, watermelon

GINGEROL • ginger

PREBIOTICS • apples, bananas, cucumbers, flaxseed, mango, pineapple, watermelon

PROBIOTICS • Greek yogurt, kefir, kombucha

Probiotic Rosemary–Kefir Tonic

Kefir is a beverage made from fermented milk. It has a slightly tart taste that balances the acidity of oranges and sweetness of maple syrup.

RECIPE TYPE
- steeped then shaken

HEAVY-HITTING NUTRIENTS
- probiotics

Makes 1½ cups (350 ml) or 6 shots
One shot: ¼ cup (60 ml)

- 1¼ cups (300 ml) water
- 1 fresh rosemary sprig
- 1 navel orange, cut into 8 wedges
- ½ cup (125 ml) low-fat plain kefir
- 2 teaspoons (10 ml) pure maple syrup

1. Combine the water, rosemary, and orange wedges in a small saucepan and bring to a boil over high heat. Remove pan from the heat and set aside, covered, for 15 minutes to allow the flavors to blend. Uncover and allow to cool for 10 minutes.

2. Strain the liquid into a bowl and discard the solids. Pour the strained liquid, kefir, and maple syrup into the bowl and whisk for 30 seconds, until well combined. Pour up to 3 shots into a glass and serve.

To store, cool, then pour into an airtight container, cover, and place in the refrigerator for up to 4 days. Alternatively, pour shots into ice cube trays, cover or store in a freezer bag, and freeze for up to 2 months. Always label and date your tonics.

If you don't have kefir, use plain low-fat yogurt.

Digestion-Boosting Shots

People have long talked about the health benefits of apple cider vinegar. Research hasn't backed up these claims, but there are many anecdotes, especially regarding how it helps digestion—and here it gives this tasty shot some extra zing!

RECIPE TYPE
- juiced

HEAVY-HITTING NUTRIENTS
- gingerol, prebiotics

Makes 1½ cups (350 ml) or 6 shots
One shot: ¼ cup (60 ml)

- 3 cups (495 g) cubed pineapple
- 2-inch (5 cm) piece ginger
- 1 tablespoon (15 ml) apple cider vinegar

1. Place the pineapple, ginger, and vinegar in a juicer and juice.

2. Pour up to 3 shots into a glass and serve.

To store, pour into an airtight container, cover, and place in the refrigerator for up to 4 days. Alternatively, pour shots into ice cube trays, cover or store in a freezer bag, and freeze for up to 2 months. Always label and date your tonics.

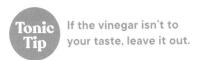 **Tonic Tip** If the vinegar isn't to your taste, leave it out.

Prebiotic Watermelon– Flax Shots

Watermelon is a refreshing prebiotic that helps foster the growth of the beneficial bacteria in the gut.

RECIPE TYPE
- juiced then shaken

HEAVY-HITTING NUTRIENTS
- prebiotics

Makes 1½ cups (350 ml) or 6 shots
One shot: ¼ cup (60 ml)

- 2 cups (304 g) cubed watermelon
- ½ Granny Smith apple, cut in half
- 1 teaspoon (3 g) ground flaxseed

1. Place the watermelon and apple in the juicer and juice.

2. Combine the juice and flaxseed in a container with a tight-fitting lid. Cover and shake for about 15 seconds, or until combined. Pour up to 3 shots into a glass and serve.

To store, pour into an airtight container, cover, and place in the refrigerator for up to 4 days. Alternatively, pour shots into ice cube trays, cover or store in a freezer bag, and freeze for up to 2 months. Always label and date your tonics.

Tonic Tip Flaxseed is sold whole and ground. Whole flaxseed is best to top salads or cooked vegetables, while ground flaxseed is best for liquids like this tonic, sauces, or dressings.

Gut–Healthy Yogurt Tonic

Yogurt has live, active microorganisms that act as probiotics, and cucumbers provide a healthy dose of water. Put the two together for a cool, refreshing, gut-healthy tonic.

RECIPE TYPE
- blended

HEAVY-HITTING NUTRIENTS
- prebiotics, probiotics

Makes 1 cup (250 ml) or 4 shots
One shot: ¼ cup (60 ml)

- ½ English or hothouse cucumber, cut into large chunks
- Juice of 1 lime
- ½ cup (125 ml) plain nonfat Greek yogurt
- 2 teaspoons (10 ml) honey
- 6 fresh mint leaves for garnish

Place the cucumber, lime juice, yogurt, and honey in a blender and blend on high for 1 minute, or until smooth. Pour 2 shots into two glasses and serve, or up to 3 shots for one serving, saving the rest. Garnish with mint leaves.

To store, pour into an airtight container, cover, and place in the refrigerator for up to 4 days. Alternatively, pour shots into ice cube trays, cover or store in a freezer bag, and freeze for up to 2 months. Always label and date your tonics.

Tonic Tip

English cucumbers (also called hothouse) and Kirby cucumbers are soft-skinned and seedless, making them perfect for the blender.

Kombucha–Cranberry Digestion Tonic

Kombucha is a fermented beverage made from tea, sugar, bacteria, and yeast. It provides live, active cultures that may act as probiotics. Add a few gut-healthy ingredients to get the ultimate tonic for digestive health.

RECIPE TYPE
- shaken

HEAVY-HITTING NUTRIENTS
- gingerol, probiotics

Makes 1½ cups (350 ml) or 6 shots
One shot: ¼ cup (60 ml)

- 1¼ cups (300 ml) citrus-flavored kombucha
- ⅓ cup (75 ml) 100% cranberry juice
- Juice of 1 lime
- ⅛ teaspoon (0.5 g) ground ginger

Whisk together the kombucha, cranberry juice, lime juice, and ginger in a medium bowl. Pour up to 3 shots into a glass and serve.

To store, pour into an airtight container, cover, and place in the refrigerator for up to 2 days. Always label and date your tonics.

Compare kombucha nutrition facts panels and choose one with less added sugar. A citrus flavor like blood orange, lemon, or grapefruit will complement the other ingredients.

Calm-Gut Smoothie Shots

Greek yogurt has a thick consistency and tart flavor. It contains live, active cultures that may act as probiotics, and it gives your smoothie a creamy consistency and delicious flavor.

RECIPE TYPE
• blended

HEAVY-HITTING NUTRIENTS
• prebiotics, probiotics

Makes 2 cups (500 ml) or 4 shots
One shot: ½ cup (125 ml)

- 1 medium banana
- 1 cup (150 g) frozen mango slices
- ½ cup (125 ml) plain low-fat Greek yogurt
- ¾ cup (175 ml) low-fat milk (see Tip)
- 1 tablespoon (15 ml) pure maple syrup
- 2 teaspoons (5 g) ground flaxseed

Place the banana, mango, yogurt, milk, maple syrup, and flaxseed in a blender and blend on high for 1 minute, or until smooth. Pour up to 2 shots into a glass and serve immediately.

This is best consumed immediately as the texture changes quickly, so no storage instructions here. If you need only 2 shots, halve the recipe.

Tonic Tip To get even more probiotics, swap the milk for plain low-fat kefir. Many plant-based and lactose-free yogurts contain live, active cultures that act as probiotics. Check the label.

Chapter 7

Calming Shots

RECIPES

Anti-Anxiety Overview

There is growing scientific evidence of a connection between mental health and diet. One area of study includes the gut-brain connection. Your gut microbiome houses trillions of microorganisms including bacteria, viruses, and fungi. These microorganisms support various brain functions such as cognition, hormone production, and mood, and also play a role in helping fight infection and build immunity. When you eat a healthy, balanced diet, your gut breaks down foods and creates short-chain fatty acids, which help regulate your immune system, protect your brain and heart, and fight inflammation. Inflammation has been identified as a trigger to chemical reactions in the body that can impact brain function and mood regulation. A diet rich in fruits, vegetables, whole grains, nuts, and seeds can help reduce inflammation and ultimately may help reduce symptoms of depression.

Below is a list of top nutrients that may contribute to a calmer mind and body and some of the foods and beverages in which they are found.

· ·

CURCUMIN · turmeric

FLAVANOLS · unsweetened cocoa powder

FOLATE · beets, parsley, spinach, strawberries

GINGEROL · ginger

L-THEANINE · green tea

MAGNESIUM · almond milk, almond butter, beets, unsweetened cocoa powder

POTASSIUM · apples, grapefruit, beets

TRITERPENES · reishi mushrooms

TRYPTOPHAN · unsweetened oat milk, cashew milk

VITAMIN C · apples, grapefruit, parsley

Stress-Relieving Grapefruit and Greens Tonic

Research reveals that low levels of folate can contribute to symptoms of anxiety and stress. Spinach and grapefruit are brimming with folate, and in this tasty tonic, they're combined with foods that provide other nutrients linked to helping reduce stress.

RECIPE TYPE
- juiced

HEAVY-HITTING NUTRIENTS
- folate, gingerol, vitamin C

Makes 1½ cups (350 ml) or 6 shots
One shot: ¼ cup (60 ml)

- 2 cups (60 g) baby spinach leaves
- ½ pink or red grapefruit, peeled and divided into sections
- 1 Granny Smith apple, quartered
- 1 rib celery, cut into large chunks
- 1 Kirby or mini cucumber, cut into large chunks
- 2-inch (5 cm) piece fresh ginger

Place the spinach, grapefruit, apple, celery, cucumber, and ginger in a juicer and juice. Pour up to 3 shots into a glass and serve.

Store as you would all cold health shots.

 Tonic Tip Other folate-filled foods to add to your meals are beans, peanuts, and whole grains.

Stress-Reducing Mushroom Tonic

"Adaptogenic" is a term for foods, herbs, roots, and other plant substances—like mushrooms—that help our bodies manage stress and restore balance. In this warming tonic, the umami flavor of the mushrooms balances the sweetness of oat milk. Look for dried mushrooms in a specialty or Asian market.

RECIPE TYPE
- steeped then shaken

HEAVY-HITTING NUTRIENTS
- triterpenes, tryptophan

Makes 1 cup (250 ml) or 4 shots
One shot: ¼ cup (60 ml)

- ½ cup (125 ml) dried reishi mushrooms
- ¾ cup (175 ml) water
- ½ cup (125 ml) unsweetened oat milk
- 1 tablespoon (15 ml) pure maple syrup

1. Combine the mushrooms and water in a small saucepan and bring to a boil over high heat. Remove pan from the heat and set aside, covered, for 20 minutes.

2. Strain the liquid into a bowl and discard the solids. Combine the strained liquid, oat milk, and maple syrup in a container with a tight-fitting lid. Cover and shake the container for 15 seconds, or until well combined.

3. Pour up to 2 shots into a small mug or heatproof glass and serve warm or at room temperature.

(recipe continues)

To store, cool, then pour into an airtight container, cover, and place in the refrigerator for up to 4 days. Alternatively, pour shots into ice cube trays, cover or store in a freezer bag, and freeze for up to 2 months. Always label and date your tonics.

To reheat, defrost if necessary and place a shot in a small saucepan and bring to a boil over high heat, stirring occasionally. Remove pan from the heat and allow tonic to cool slightly. Pour into a small mug or heatproof glass and serve.

 Swap the reishi mushrooms for lion's mane mushrooms or dried cordyceps.

Golden Milk Calming Shots

This soothing warm tonic originated in India and is a go-to solution for many ailments, including restlessness. The comforting effect could be due to the curcumin found in turmeric.

RECIPE TYPE
- steeped

HEAVY-HITTING NUTRIENTS
- curcumin, gingerol, magnesium

Makes 1 cup (250 ml) or 4 shots
One shot: ¼ cup (60 ml)

- ½ cup (125 ml) unsweetened coconut milk, divided
- 2 teaspoons (11 g) almond butter
- 1 teaspoon (5 ml) honey
- ¼ teaspoon (1 g) ground ginger
- ⅛ teaspoon (0.5 ml) pure vanilla extract
- ⅛ teaspoon (0.5 g) ground cinnamon
- ⅛ teaspoon (0.5 g) ground turmeric
- Pinch of ground black pepper
- ½ cup (125 ml) unsweetened almond milk

1. Place ¼ cup (60 ml) of the coconut milk in a small saucepan and warm over low heat.

2. Whisk in the almond butter, honey, ginger, vanilla, cinnamon, turmeric, and black pepper until combined. Increase the heat to medium and slowly whisk in the remaining ¼ cup (60 ml) coconut milk and all the almond milk. Continue cooking, whisking occasionally, for 3 minutes. Set aside to cool slightly.

3. Pour up to 2 shots into a small mug or heatproof glass and serve warm.

(recipe continues)

To store, cool, then pour into an airtight container, cover, and place in the refrigerator for up to 4 days. Alternatively, pour shots into ice cube trays, cover or store in a freezer bag, and freeze for up to 2 months. Always label and date your tonics.

To reheat, defrost if necessary, then pour into a small saucepan and bring to a boil over high heat, stirring occasionally. Remove pan from the heat and allow tonic to cool slightly. Pour into a small mug or heatproof glass and serve.

 The pinch of black pepper enhances the absorption of curcumin, the active compound in turmeric.

Peaceful Dark Cocoa Blend

Vitamin C along with components in dark chocolate can help control cortisol levels and may reduce stress. Plus, who doesn't love the delicious combination of strawberries and chocolate?

RECIPE TYPE
- blended

HEAVY-HITTING NUTRIENTS
- flavanols, folate, magnesium, vitamin C

Makes 1½ cups (350 ml) or 6 shots
One shot: ¼ cup (60 ml)

- 1 cup (250 ml) unsweetened almond milk
- 1 cup (150 g) fresh strawberries, trimmed
- 1 tablespoon (5 g) unsweetened cocoa powder
- 2 teaspoons (10 ml) honey

Place the almond milk, strawberries, cocoa powder, and honey in a blender and blend on high for 1 minute, or until smooth. Pour up to 3 shots into a glass and serve.

To store, pour into an airtight container, cover, and place in the refrigerator for up to 4 days. Alternatively, pour shots into ice cube trays, cover or store in a freezer bag, and freeze for up to 2 months. Always label and date your tonics.

 Tonic Tip To avoid mold growth on strawberries, wash only before using or eating (not before storing).

Soothing Chai-Cashew Elixir

Chai contains the amino acid L-theanine, which may help reduce stress and anxiety and promote relaxation. It's a soothing tonic you can enjoy any time.

RECIPE TYPE
- steeped

HEAVY-HITTING NUTRIENTS
- magnesium, L-theanine

Makes 1 cup (250 ml) or 4 shots
One shot: ¼ cup (60 ml)

- 1¼ cups (300 ml) unsweetened cashew milk
- 4 black peppercorns
- 2 whole cloves
- 2 cinnamon sticks
- 1-inch (2.5 cm) piece fresh ginger
- 2 chai tea bags

1. Combine the cashew milk, peppercorns, cloves, cinnamon, and ginger in a small saucepan and bring to a boil over high heat. Add the tea bags. Remove pan from the heat and allow the tea to steep, covered, for 4 minutes. Carefully remove the tea bags and discard. Re-cover the pan and let stand for 15 minutes to allow the flavors to blend.

2. Strain the tea into a small bowl and discard the solids. Pour up to 2 shots into a small mug or heatproof glass and serve warm.

To store, cool, then pour into an airtight container, cover, and place in the refrigerator for up to 4 days. Alternatively, pour shots into ice cube trays, cover or store in a freezer bag, and freeze for up to 2 months. Always label and date your tonics.

To reheat, defrost if necessary, then pour the shot into a small saucepan and bring to a boil over high heat, whisking occasionally. Remove pan from the heat and allow tonic to cool slightly. Pour into a small mug or heatproof glass and serve.

 Store any extra fresh ginger in an airtight container or sealed bag in the refrigerator for up to 1 month.

Relaxing Beet Blend

Some research correlates anxiety with a low-antioxidant level. Beets and limes are two great sources of antioxidants and are tailor-made for relaxation.

RECIPE TYPE
* juiced

HEAVY-HITTING NUTRIENTS
* folate, magnesium, vitamin C

Makes 1½ cups (350 ml) or 6 shots
One shot: ¼ cup (60 ml)

- 1 red beet, trimmed and quartered
- 1 Granny Smith apple, quartered
- 1 cup (30 g) fresh flat leaf or curly parsley
- 2 Kirby or mini cucumbers, cut into chunks
- 1 lime, peeled and halved

1. Place the beet, apple, parsley, cucumbers, and lime in a juicer and juice.
2. Pour up to 3 shots into a glass and serve.

To store, pour into an airtight container, cover, and place in the refrigerator for up to 4 days. Alternatively, pour shots into ice cube trays, cover or store in a freezer bag, and freeze for up to 2 months. Always label and date your tonics.

 Beets can and do stain! To help remove stains on your hands, cut a lemon in half and rub the cut side on the stained skin.

Shots for Healthy Skin, Nails, and Hair

RECIPES

Overview for Healthy Skin, Nails, and Hair

Genetics and hormones play a large role in the appearance of your skin, hair, and nails—but so does what you eat. Instead of buying all the latest lotions and potions, why not start with what's on your plate and in your glass? It's a whole lot cheaper! The work of free radicals—highly reactive and unstable molecules that damage cells—can manifest in skin as wrinkles, thickening, discoloration, and decreased elasticity; in nails as ridges, splitting, and brittleness. And over time, free radicals may make hair dry, dull, or brittle and cause decreased growth rate and possibly even hair loss. This chapter is filled with tonics containing ingredients with antioxidants that can help stabilize free radicals and minimize or decrease damage.

Below is a list of top nutrients that may promote healthy skin, nails, and hair and some of the foods and beverages in which they are found.

....

ANTHOCYANINS • pomegranate juice, raspberries

BETA-CAROTENE • carrots

BIOTIN • avocados

CATECHINS • green tea

FOLATE • avocados, pomegranate juice

GINGEROL • ginger

LYCOPENE • tomatoes

MAGNESIUM • cantaloupe

VITAMIN A • carrots, tomatoes

VITAMIN B6 • cantaloupe, pineapple

VITAMIN C • apples, avocados, cantaloupe, cucumbers, kiwis, lemons, oranges, pomegranate juice, raspberries, watermelon

VITAMIN E • avocados, kiwis

Hair-Enhancing Pineapple-Kiwi Tonic

Pineapple and kiwi are brimming with the antioxidant vitamin C that can help form collagen. Plus, the combination of the sweet and tart flavors of these two fruits is unbelievably delicious!

RECIPE TYPE
- juiced

HEAVY-HITTING NUTRIENTS
- vitamin B6, vitamin C, vitamin E

Makes 1 cup (250 ml) or 4 shots
One shot: ¼ cup (60 ml)

- 1 cup (165 g) cubed pineapple
- 2 Kirby or mini cucumbers, cut into chunks
- 1 kiwi, halved

Place the pineapple, cucumbers, and kiwi in a juicer and juice. Pour up to 2 shots into a glass and serve.

To store, pour into an airtight container, cover, and place in the refrigerator for up to 4 days. Alternatively, pour shots into ice cube trays, cover or store in a freezer bag, and freeze for up to 2 months. Always label and date your tonics.

Tonic Tip Either green- or gold-fleshed kiwi can be used in this tonic.

Healthy Skin-and-Hair Cucumber Tonic

Consuming fruits and vegetables help keep the skin hydrated. The vitamin C in the cantaloupe helps with collagen production for healthy skin, nails, and hair. The sweet cantaloupe balanced with the cooling mint makes this tonic delicious and refreshing.

RECIPE TYPE
- juiced

HEAVY-HITTING NUTRIENTS
- magnesium, vitamin B6, vitamin C

Makes 1½ cups (350 ml) or 6 shots
One shot: ¼ cup (60 ml)

- 2 cups (320 g) cubed cantaloupe
- ½ English or hothouse cucumber, cut into chunks
- ¼ cup (8 g) fresh mint leaves

Place the cantaloupe, cucumber, and mint in a juicer and juice. Pour up to 3 shots into a glass and serve.

To store, pour into an airtight container, cover, and place in the refrigerator for up to 4 days. Alternatively, pour shots into ice cube trays, cover or store in a freezer bag, and freeze for up to 2 months. Always label and date your tonics.

Tonic Tip

Cantaloupe also tastes great in a smoothie or fruit salad, or paired with savory and salty foods like prosciutto.

Tonic for Strong Nails

Avocados are brimming with nutrients, and their healthy unsaturated fat helps with absorption of the fat-soluble vitamins they contain. Green tea is also filled with powerful antioxidants that can help prevent brittle nails.

RECIPE TYPE
- steeped then blended

HEAVY-HITTING NUTRIENTS
- biotin, catechins, folate, vitamin C, vitamin E

Makes 1½ cups (350 ml) or 6 shots
One shot: ¼ cup (60 ml)

- 1 green tea bag
- 1½ cups (350 ml) boiling water
- 1 avocado, pitted
- 1 tablespoon (60 ml) pure maple syrup

1. Place the tea bag in a large mug and add boiling water. Steep for exactly 3 minutes, then remove the tea bag and discard. Allow the tea to cool slightly (you don't want to put hot liquid in a blender—it'll explode).

2. Place the tea, avocado, and maple syrup in a blender and blend on high for 1 minute until smooth. Pour up to 3 shots into a glass and serve warm or at room temperature.

To store, cool, pour into an airtight container, cover, and place in the refrigerator for up to 4 days. Alternatively, pour shots into ice cube trays, cover or store in a freezer bag, and freeze for up to 2 months. Always label and date your tonics.

 Tonic Tip

A ripe avocado will yield to pressure and have a darker peel than an unripe one. Overripe avocados are mushy or have deep indentations.

Glowing-Skin Tonic

Beta-carotene found in carrots and oranges can benefit skin health, and here they combine to make a delicious, photo-worthy tonic.

RECIPE TYPE
- juiced

HEAVY-HITTING NUTRIENTS
- beta-carotene, vitamin C

Makes 1½ cups (350 ml) or 6 shots
One shot: ¼ cup (60 ml)

- 2 medium carrots, cut into chunks
- 2 navel oranges, peeled and quartered
- 1 medium red apple (such as Fuji, Gala, Honeycrisp, Pink Lady, or Envy), quartered

Place the carrots, oranges, and apple in a juicer and juice. Pour up to 3 shots into a glass and serve.

To store, pour into an airtight container, cover, and place in the refrigerator for up to 4 days. Alternatively, pour shots into ice cube trays, cover or store in a freezer bag, and freeze for up to 2 months. Always label and date your tonics.

 Tonic Tip Swap 4 mandarins for the 2 navel oranges. They are also brimming with vitamin C.

Skin-Protecting Elixir

Hydration, hydration, hydration—it helps keep your skin plump and smooth. Both watermelon and tomatoes are filled with water and a healthy amount of the antioxidant vitamin C, which also helps with collagen production.

RECIPE TYPE
• juiced

HEAVY-HITTING NUTRIENTS
• lycopene, vitamin A, vitamin C

Makes 1½ cups (350 ml) or 6 shots
One shot: ¼ cup (60 ml)

- 1 cup (152 g) cubed watermelon
- 1 beefsteak tomato, quartered

Place the watermelon and tomato in a juicer and juice. Pour up to 3 shots into a glass and serve.

To store, pour into an airtight container, cover, and place in the refrigerator for up to 4 days. Alternatively, pour shots into ice cube trays, cover or store in a freezer bag, and freeze for up to 2 months. Always label and date your tonics.

To store extra tonic, pour shots of the mixture into individual containers or the remaining mixture into one large container, cover, and place in the refrigerator for up to 4 days. Label and date the container.

 Beefsteak tomatoes are large, plump, meaty tomatoes that are commonly found at your local supermarket year-round, and when they're in season in late summer, you'll find them at farmers markets. You can use either for this tonic.

Dewy-Skin Pomegranate Shots

Pomegranate juice is made with the rind, pith, and peel of the fruit, in addition to the arils—which is the more technically correct name for the seeds. Some animal research has connected the consumption of the pomegranate peel with protection from UVB rays. The anthocyanins found in the pomegranate juice and raspberries may also help protect the skin from UV light.

RECIPE TYPE
- steeped

HEAVY-HITTING NUTRIENTS
- anthocyanins, folate, gingerol, vitamin C

Makes 1 cup (250 ml) or 4 shots
One shot: ¼ cup (60 ml)

- ¾ cup (175 ml) 100% pomegranate juice
- ¼ cup (60 ml) freshly squeezed lemon juice
- ½ cup (62 g) fresh or defrosted raspberries
- 2-inch (5 cm) piece fresh ginger, cut into chunks

1. Combine the pomegranate juice, lemon juice, raspberries, and ginger in a small saucepan and bring to a boil over high heat. Reduce the heat to low and cook, covered, about 10 minutes to ensure the flavors combine. Allow to cool slightly.

2. Strain the liquid into a bowl and discard the solids. Pour up to 2 shots into a heatproof glass or small mug and serve warm or at room temperature.

(recipe continues)

To store, cool, then pour into an airtight container, cover, and place in the refrigerator for up to 4 days. Alternatively, pour shots into ice cube trays, cover or store in a freezer bag, and freeze for up to 2 months. Always label and date your tonics.

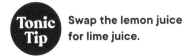 **Swap the lemon juice for lime juice.**

Chapter 9

Energizing Shots

RECIPES

Energy Overview

Although many folks are looking for easy ways to increase energy, many "energy" drinks fall under the category of supplements, which the FDA has only limited authority to regulate. Some of these drinks contain stimulants like guarana, which is much stronger than the better-known stimulant, caffeine. Although drinking 3 to 4 cups (700 to 950 ml) of coffee or black tea per day can be safe (no more than 400 milligrams of caffeine), too much caffeine or other stimulants can lead to symptoms like a rapid or irregular heartbeat, change in focus, breathing trouble, agitation, seizures, diarrhea, dizziness, fever, increased thirst and urination, and muscle twitching. This is because stimulants affect the brain and nervous systems.

So, what gives you energy in a healthy and safe way? Simple carbohydrates like honey, milk, or fruit will give you a boost. The tonics in this chapter contain a combo of simple carbs and a little caffeine.

Below is a list of top energy-boosting nutrients and some of the foods and beverages in which they are found, as well as sources for caffeine.

CAFFEINE • black tea, coffee, unsweetened cocoa powder

SIMPLE CARBOHYDRATES • bananas, honey, maple syrup, milk, unsweetened oat milk, strawberries

FOLATE • avocados, spinach

PANTOTHENIC ACID • avocados

VITAMIN B6 • peanut butter

Black Tea Pick-Me-Up

Black tea provides caffeine, and when combined with the natural sugars from the pomegranate juice, these are easily digestible calories that will give you energy.

RECIPE TYPE	HEAVY-HITTING NUTRIENTS
• steeped	• caffeine, simple carbohydrates

Makes 1 cup (250 ml) or 4 cups
One shot: ¼ cup (60 ml)

- 1 cup (250 ml) water
- 1 black tea bag
- 2 tablespoons (30 ml) 100% pomegranate juice
- 2 tablespoons (30 ml) freshly squeezed lime juice
- 1 tablespoon (11 g) pomegranate arils (seeds)

1. Bring the water to a boil over high heat in a small saucepan. Turn off the heat, add the tea bag, and steep for exactly 4 minutes. Carefully remove the tea bag and discard.

2. Stir the pomegranate juice, lime juice, and arils into the tea and bring to a boil over high heat. Remove the pan from the heat and allow the mixture to cool for 10 minutes.

3. Pour up to 2 shots into a mug or heatproof glass, adding some of the pomegranate arils (seeds) from the pan. Serve immediately.

To store, cool, then pour into an airtight container, cover, and place in the refrigerator for up to 4 days. Alternatively, pour shots into ice cube trays, cover or store in a freezer bag, and freeze for up to 2 months. Always label and date your tonics.

To reheat, defrost if necessary, then pour the shot into a small saucepan and bring to a boil over high heat, whisking occasionally. Remove pan from the heat and allow tonic to cool slightly. Pour into a small mug or heatproof glass and serve.

 Pomegranates are in season during the fall; also, the seeds are often sold separately. If you can't find them, leave them out.

Energizing Chocolate– Coffee Shots

Caffeine is a stimulant, which means it increases the activity in your brain and nervous system. A shot of this tonic with caffeine from the coffee and cocoa can help increase the stimulation your body feels, while the calories in the easily digestible honey and milk will give you quick energy.

RECIPE TYPE
- steeped

HEAVY-HITTING NUTRIENTS
- caffeine, simple carbohydrates

Makes 1½ cups (350 ml) or 6 shots
One shot: ¼ cup (60 ml)

- 1¼ cups (300 ml) brewed coffee
- ¼ cup (60 ml) low-fat milk or plant-based milk of choice
- 1 tablespoon (5 g) unsweetened cocoa powder
- 2 teaspoons (10 ml) honey

1. Combine the coffee and milk in a small saucepan and bring to a boil over high heat. Reduce the heat to medium-low and add the cocoa powder and honey, whisking to combine. Continue cooking for 3 minutes more. Allow to cool to taste.

2. Pour up to 3 shots into a small mug or heatproof glass and serve warm.

(recipe continues)

To store, cool, then pour into an airtight container, cover, and place in the refrigerator for up to 4 days. Alternatively, pour shots into ice cube trays, cover or store in a freezer bag, and freeze for up to 2 months. Always label and date your tonics.

To reheat, defrost if necessary, then pour the shot into a small saucepan and bring to a boil over high heat, whisking occasionally. Remove pan from the heat and allow tonic to cool slightly. Pour into a small mug or heatproof glass and serve.

Use whichever type of milk—cow or plant— with any fat level you like. Whole milk makes a richer and higher-calorie drink. As long as it provides calories, you'll get some energy.

Revitalizing Berry Tonic

Berries and citrus fruits like lemons and limes provide vitamin C. Research has connected a lack of vitamin C to fatigue—so enjoy this delicious tonic to add more zip to your day! As always, pair your shots with a healthy diet to reap the rewards.

RECIPE TYPE
• steeped

HEAVY-HITTING NUTRIENTS
• simple carbohydrates

Makes 1 cup (250 ml) or 4 shots
One shot: ¼ cup (60 ml)

- 1¼ cups (300 ml) water
- 2 tablespoons (30 ml) fresh lime juice
- ½ cup (83 g) sliced strawberries fresh or defrosted
- ¼ cup (37 g) blueberries fresh or defrosted
- ¼ cup (31 g) raspberries fresh or defrosted

1. Place the water and lime juice in a small saucepan and bring to a boil over high heat. Remove pan from the heat and stir in the strawberries, blueberries, and raspberries. Set aside, covered, for 15 minutes.

2. Strain the liquid into a bowl and discard the solids. Pour up to 2 shots into a small mug or heatproof glass and serve warm.

(recipe continues)

To store, cool, then pour into an airtight container, cover, and place in the refrigerator for up to 4 days. Alternatively, pour shots into ice cube trays, cover or store in a freezer bag, and freeze for up to 2 months. Always label and date your tonics.

To reheat, defrost if necessary, then pour the shot into a small saucepan and bring to a boil over high heat, whisking occasionally. Remove pan from the heat and allow tonic to cool slightly. Pour into a small mug or heatproof glass and serve.

Replace the lime juice with orange or lemon juice.

Smooth Energy Shots

The avocado provides several B vitamins, including folate and vitamin B6, to help the body with energy production, and it gives this tonic its creamy, luscious texture.

RECIPE TYPE
- blended

HEAVY-HITTING NUTRIENTS
- simple carbohydrates, folate, pantothenic acid, vitamin B6

Makes 1 cup (250 ml) or 4 shots
One shot: ¼ cup (60 ml)

- 2 Kirby or mini cucumbers, cut into chunks
- 1 medium avocado, pitted and peeled
- ¾ cup (175 ml) low-fat milk or plant-based milk
- 1 tablespoon (15 ml) pure maple syrup

Place the cucumbers, avocado, milk, and maple syrup in a blender and blend on high for 1 minute, or until smooth. Pour up to 3 shots into a glass and serve.

To store, pour into an airtight container, cover, and place in the refrigerator for up to 4 days. Alternatively, pour shots into ice cube trays, cover or store in a freezer bag, and freeze for up to 2 months. Always label and date your tonics.

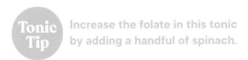

Tonic Tip

Increase the folate in this tonic by adding a handful of spinach.

Banana–Walnut Energizer

Bananas offer a variety of simple sugars that can help provide a quick source of energy. Combined with earthy walnuts and subtly sweet oat milk, it's a delicious, energizing tonic.

RECIPE TYPE
- blended

HEAVY-HITTING NUTRIENTS
- simple carbohydrates

Makes 1½ cups (350 ml) or 6 shots
One shot: ¼ cup (60 ml)

- 1 medium banana, cut into chunks
- 1 cup (250 ml) unsweetened oat milk
- ¼ cup (25 g) raw walnuts

Place the banana, oat milk, and walnuts in a blender and blend on high for 1 minute until smooth. Pour up to 3 shots into a glass and serve.

To store, pour into an airtight container, cover, and place in the refrigerator for up to 4 days. Alternatively, pour shots into ice cube trays, cover or store in a freezer bag, and freeze for up to 2 months. Always label and date your tonics.

 Tonic Tip Place shelled or unshelled walnuts in an airtight container and store in the refrigerator to keep them fresh.

Peanut Butter Power Elixir

The amino acid tyrosine in peanut butter and the folate in leafy green vegetables help maintain good energy levels and nerve function in helping fight fatigue. Plus, everything tastes better with peanut butter!

RECIPE TYPE
- blended

HEAVY-HITTING NUTRIENTS
- folate, simple carbohydrates, vitamin B6

Makes 1½ cups (350 ml) or 6 shots
One shot: ¼ cup (60 ml)

- 2 cups (60 g) baby spinach leaves
- 1½ cups (350 ml) unsweetened oat milk
- 1 tablespoon (16 g) smooth peanut butter
- 2 teaspoons (10 ml) pure maple syrup

Place the spinach, oat milk, peanut butter, and maple syrup in a blender and blend on high for 1 minute, or until smooth. Pour up to 3 shots into a glass and serve.

To store, pour into an airtight container, cover, and place in the refrigerator for up to 4 days. Alternatively, pour shots into ice cube trays, cover or store in a freezer bag, and freeze for up to 2 months. Always label and date your tonics.

Tonic Tip
To make life easier, purchase packaged baby spinach that's been prewashed.

Index

Acknowledgments

This book came together thanks to an amazing team of folks. First and foremost, I would like to thank my literary agent, Sally Ekus, who has believed in me for over ten years. Also, a big thank-you to my editors Kylie Foxx McDonald and Mary Ellen O'Neill who were a pleasure to work with on this fun and timely topic.

A huge thank-you to the book designers Galen Smith and Becky Terhune, art director Suet Chong, photographer Leesa Renae of Plated Productions, publicity and marketing experts Rebecca Carlisle and Moira Kerrigan, production editor Kate Karol, and HBG's enthusiastic sales team.

Last but certainly not least, I would like to thank my children, Schoen, Ellena, and Micah who are always there to support me—especially when I had to work weekends to get my recipe testing done. I love you all very much!